ANIMAL Hats & Scarves

Meet Michele Maks:

A crochet and knit designer since 1985, Michele Maks has lost count of the creations she has made, but she hasn't lost her enthusiasm.

"The next project is always the most exciting!" she says. "I never work on one thing at a time. I'm probably most fascinated by (dare I say it?) granny squares!"

Her designs have appeared in magazines, books, and yarn industry publications. A diagnosis of multiple sclerosis in 2009 hasn't stopped her. "Crochet has been a constant solace in battling the effects of this disease," she says.

Her online subscription service offers digital patterns for all skill levels at MainlyCrochet.org. She also blogs and is active on social media.

BONUS!

LOOK FOR THE CAMERA
in our instructions and watch our technique videos made just for you!
www.LeisureArts.com/6731

LEISURE ARTS, INC. • Maumelle, Arkansas

BEAR

EASY +

SHOPPING LIST

Yarn (Medium Weight) MEDIUM 4
[5 ounces, 251 yards
(142 grams, 230 meters) per skein]:

Scarf

☐ MC (Brown) - 1 skein

Hat

☐ MC (Brown) - 1 skein

(Bulky Weight Eyelash) BULKY 5
[1.75 ounces, 64 yards
(50 grams, 58 meters) per skein]:

Scarf

☐ CC (Brown) - 2 skeins

Hat

☐ CC (Brown) - 1{2-2} skein(s)

Crochet Hooks

☐ Size J (6 mm) **and**

☐ Size M/N (9 mm)

or sizes needed for gauge

Additional Supplies

☐ Yarn needle

SIZE INFORMATION

Scarf

Finished Size:

3½" wide x 32½{40-47½}" long/
9 cm x 82.5{101.5-120.5 cm
and 6" (15 cm) width at paws

Hat

Size: Small{Medium-Large}

Fits Head Circumference:

16{18-21}"/40.5{45.5-53.5} cm

Size Note: We have printed the instructions for the sizes in different colors to make it easier for you to find:

- Small in Blue
- Medium in Pink
- Large in Green

Instructions in Black apply to all sizes.

GAUGE INFORMATION

With larger size hook and holding one strand each of MC and CC together,
9 sc and 9 rows = 3½" (9 cm)

Gauge Swatch: 3½" (9 cm) square

With larger size hook, holding one strand each of MC and CC together, ch 10.

Row 1: Sc in second ch from hook and in each ch across: 9 sc.

Rows 2-9: Ch 1, turn; sc in each sc across.

Finish off.

STITCH GUIDE

DOUBLE TREBLE CROCHET

(abbreviated dtr)

YO 3 times, insert hook in sc indicated, YO and pull up a loop (5 loops on hook), (YO and draw through 2 loops on hook) 4 times.

SINGLE CROCHET 2 TOGETHER

(abbreviated sc2tog)

Pull up a loop in each of next 2 sc, YO and draw through all 3 loops on hook **(counts as one sc)**.

SINGLE CROCHET 3 TOGETHER

(abbreviated sc3tog)

Pull up a loop in each of next 3 sc, YO and draw through all 4 loops on hook **(counts as one sc)**.

SCARF

With larger size hook and holding one strand each of MC and CC together, ch 10.

Row 1: Sc in second ch from hook and in each ch across: 9 sc.

Rows 2-4: Ch 1, turn; 2 sc in first sc, sc in each sc across to last sc, 2 sc in last sc: 15 sc.

Rows 5-12: Ch 1, turn; sc in each sc across.

Rows 13-15: Ch 1, turn; beginning in first sc, sc2tog, sc in each sc across last 2 sc, sc2tog: 9 sc.

Row 16: Ch 1, turn; sc in each sc across.

Repeat Row 16 until piece measures approximately 27{34½-42}"/ 68.5{87.5-106.5} cm from beginning ch.

Last 14 Rows: Repeat Rows 2-15.

Finish off.

APPLIQUÉS

LARGE PAD (Make 2)

With smaller size hook and one strand of MC, ch 12.

Row 1 (Right side)**:** Sc in second ch from hook and in each ch across: 11 sc.

Note: Loop a short piece of yarn around any stitch to mark Row 1 as **right** side.

Row 2: Ch 1, turn; sc in each sc across.

Row 3: Ch 1, turn; sc in first 2 sc, skip next 3 sc, 7 dtr in next sc, skip next 3 sc, sc in last 2 sc.

Edging: Ch 1, do **not** turn; slip st in end of each row across; working in free loops of beginning ch *(Fig. 2, page 31)*, slip st in first ch, skip next ch, 5 dc in next ch, skip next 2 chs, sc in next ch, skip next 2 chs, 5 dc in next ch, skip next ch, slip st in next ch and in end of each row across; finish off leaving a long end for sewing.

SMALL PAD (Make 10)

With smaller size hook and one strand of MC, ch 4.

Rnd 1 (Right side)**:** Sc in second ch from hook, hdc in next ch, (sc, ch 1, sc) in last ch; working in free loops of beginning ch, hdc in next ch, sc in next ch, ch 1; join with slip st to first sc, finish off leaving a long end for sewing.

Note: Mark Row 1 as **right** side.

Using photo as a guide for placement, page 5, sew one Large Pad with **right** side facing on same side of each end of Scarf. Sew 5 Small Pads with **right** side facing around each Large Pad along outer edge.

HAT

With larger size hook and holding one strand each of MC and CC together, ch 4; join with slip st to form a ring.

Rnd 1 (Right side)**:** Ch 1, 8 sc in ring; join with slip st to first sc.

Note: Mark Rnd 1 as **right** side.

Rnd 2: Ch 1, 2 sc in same st as joining and in each sc around; join with slip st to first sc: 16 sc.

Rnd 3: Ch 1, sc in same st as joining, 2 sc in next sc, (sc in next sc, 2 sc in next sc) around; join with slip st to first sc: 24 sc.

Rnd 4: Ch 1, **turn**; sc in same st as joining and in next sc, 2 sc in next sc, (sc in next 2 sc, 2 sc in next sc) around; join with slip st to first sc: 32 sc.

Size Medium ONLY

Rnd 5: Ch 1, do **not** turn; sc in same st as joining and in next 6 sc, 2 sc in next sc, (sc in next 7 sc, 2 sc in next sc) around; join with slip st to first sc: 36 sc.

Size Large ONLY

Rnd 5: Ch 1, do **not** turn; sc in same st as joining and in next 2 sc, 2 sc in next sc, (sc in next 3 sc, 2 sc in next sc) around; join with slip st to first sc: 40 sc.

Rnd 6: Ch 1, sc in same st as joining and in next 8 sc, 2 sc in next sc, (sc in next 9 sc, 2 sc in next sc) around; join with slip st to first sc: 44 sc.

All Sizes

Rnd 5{6-7}: Ch 1, do **not** turn; sc in same st as joining and in each sc around; join with slip st to first sc.

Next 8{9-10} Rnds: Ch 1, **turn**; sc in same st as joining and in each sc around; join with slip st to first sc, do **not** finish off.

FIRST EARFLAP

Row 1: Slip st in next 3{4-4} sc, ch 1, sc in same st and in next 6{6-7} sc:, leave remaining sc unworked 7{7-8} sc.

Row 2: Ch 1, turn; sc in each sc across.

Row 3: Ch 1, turn; beginning in first sc, sc2tog, sc in next 3{3-4} sc, sc2tog: 5{5-6} sc.

Row 4: Ch 1, turn; sc in each sc across.

Row 5: Ch 1, turn; beginning in first sc, sc2tog, sc in next 1{1-2} sc, sc2tog: 3{3-4} sc.

Row 6: Ch 1, turn; sc in each sc across.

Size Large ONLY

Row 7: Ch 1, turn; sc in first sc, sc2tog, sc in last sc: 3 sc.

All Sizes

Next 7{9-10} Rows: Ch 1, turn; sc in each sc across.

Last Row: Ch 1, turn; beginning in first sc, sc3tog; finish off: one sc.

SECOND EARFLAP

Row 1: With **right** side facing and holding one strand each of MC and CC together, skip next 12{14-20} sc from First Earflap, join yarn with sc in next sc *(see Joining With Sc, page 29)*; sc in next 6{6-7} sc, leave remaining sts unworked: 7{7-8} sc.

Beginning with Row 2, complete same as First Earflap.

EAR (Make 2)

OUTER EAR

With larger size hook and holding one strand each of MC and CC together, ch 7.

Row 1 (Right side)**:** Sc in second ch from hook and in each ch across: 6 sc.

Note: Mark Row 1 as **right** side.

Rows 2-4: Ch 1, turn; sc in each sc across.

Row 5: Ch 1, turn, beginning in first sc, sc2tog, sc in next 2 sc, sc2tog; finish off: 4 sc.

INNER EAR

With larger size hook and holding two strands of MC together, work same as Outer Ear.

Joining: Hold Inner and Outer Ears with **wrong** sides together and Inner Ear facing. With larger size hook, holding one strand each of MC and CC together and working through **both** thicknesses, join yarn with sc in end of Row 1; sc in end of each row across; sc in each sc across Row 5; sc in end of each row across; finish off leaving a long end of MC for sewing.

Using photo as a guide for placement, sew bottom of Ears to Hat.

FOX

EASY +

SHOPPING LIST

Yarn (Medium Weight) 4
[3.5 ounces, 170 yards
(100 grams, 156 meters) per skein]:

Scarf

- ☐ Color A (Orange) - 1 skein
- ☐ Color B (White) - 1 skein

Hat

- ☐ Color A (Orange) - 2 skeins
- ☐ Color B (White) - 1 skein

(Bulky Weight Eyelash) 5
[1.75 ounces, 64 yards
(50 grams, 58 meters) per skein]:

Scarf

- ☐ Color C (Orange) - 2 skeins
- ☐ Color D (White) - 2 skeins

Hat

- ☐ Color C (Orange) - 2 skeins
- ☐ Color D (White) - 2 skeins

Crochet Hooks

- ☐ Size J (6 mm) **and**
- ☐ Size N/P (10 mm)

or sizes needed for gauge

Additional Supplies

- ☐ Yarn needle

SIZE INFORMATION

Scarf

Finished Size:

6{7-8}" wide x 40½{45-47½}" long
15{18-20.5} cm/
103{114.5-120.5} cm

Hat

Size: Small{Medium-Large}

Fits Head Circumference:

16{18-21}"/40.5{45.5-53.5} cm

Size Note: We have printed the instructions for the sizes in different colors to make it easier for you to find:

- Small in Blue
- Medium in Pink
- Large in Green

Instructions in Black apply to all sizes.

GAUGE INFORMATION

With larger size hook and holding one strand each of Color A and Color C together,
8 dc = 4" (10 cm);
6 rows = 5½" (14 cm)

Gauge Swatch: 4" wide x 5½" high (10 cm x 14 cm)

With larger size hook and holding one strand each of Color A and Color C together, ch 10.

Row 1: Dc in fourth ch from hook (**3 skipped chs count as first dc**) and in each ch across: 8 dc.

Rows 2-6: Ch 3 (**counts as first dc**), turn; dc in next dc and in each dc across.

Finish off.

STITCH GUIDE

SINGLE CROCHET 2 TOGETHER

(abbreviated sc2tog)

Pull up a loop in each of next 2 sc, YO and draw through all 3 loops on hook (**counts as one sc**).

SINGLE CROCHET 3 TOGETHER

(abbreviated sc3tog)

Pull up a loop in each of next 3 sc, YO and draw through all 4 loops on hook (**counts as one sc**).

SCARF

With larger size hook and holding one strand each of Color B and Color D together and leaving a long end of Color B for sewing, ch 14{16-18}.

Row 1: Dc in fourth ch from hook (**3 skipped chs count as first dc**) and in each ch across: 12{14-16} dc.

Rows 2 thru 4{5-6}: Ch 3 (**counts as first dc, now and throughout**), turn; dc in next dc and in each dc across; at end of last row, change to one strand each of Color A and Color C *(Fig. 3b, page 31)*.

Row 5{6-7}: Ch 3, turn; dc in next dc and in each dc across.

Repeat Row 5{6-7} until piece measures approximately 34{38½-41}"/86.5{98-104} cm from beginning ch.

Next Row: Ch 3, turn; dc in next dc and in each dc across changing to one strand each of Color B and Color D, cut previous colors.

Last 6 Rows: Ch 3, turn; dc in next dc and in each dc across.

Finish off, leaving a long end of Color B for sewing.

Thread yarn needle with long end. Weave needle through sts on last row *(Fig. 5, page 31)*; pull tightly to close and secure end.

Thread yarn needle with long beginning end. Weave needle through free loops of beginning ch *(Fig. 2, page 31)*, pull tightly to close and secure end.

HAT

With larger size hook and holding one strand each of Color A and Color C together, work same as Bear Hat for 13{15-17} rnds, page 4: 32{36-44} sc.

Rnd 14{16-18}: Ch 1, turn; sc in first 26{26-28} sc changing to one strand each of Color B and Color D in last sc made *(Fig. 3a, page 31)*, drop previous colors; sc in last 6{10-16} sc; join with slip st to first sc.

Rnd 15{17-19}: Ch 1, turn; sc in same st as joining and in next 5{9-15} sc changing to one strand each of Color A and Color C in last sc made, drop previous colors, sc in each sc around; join with slip st to first sc, finish off Color A and Color C only.

VISOR

Size Small ONLY

Row 1: With one strand of Color B and Color D, ch 1, do **not** turn; sc in same st as joining and in next 5 sc, leave remaining sc unworked: 6 sc.

Row 2: Ch 1, turn; sc in each sc across.

Row 3: Ch 1, turn; beginning in first sc, sc2tog, sc in next 2 sc, sc2tog: 4 sc.

Row 4: Ch 1, turn; sc in each sc across.

Row 5: Ch 1, turn; beginning in first sc, sc2tog twice: 2 sc.

Row 6: Ch 1, turn; beginning in first sc, sc2tog; finish off: one sc.

Size Medium ONLY

Row 1: With one strand of Color B and Color D, ch 1, do **not** turn; sc in same st as joining and in next 9 sc, leave remaining sc unworked: 10 sc.

Row 2: Ch 1, turn; sc in each sc across.

Rows 3-5: Ch 1, turn; beginning in first sc, sc2tog, sc in each sc across to last 2 sc, sc2tog: 4 sc.

Row 6: Ch 1, turn; sc in each sc across.

Row 7: Ch 1, turn; beginning in first sc, sc2tog twice: 2 sc.

Row 8: Ch 1, turn; beginning in first sc, sc2tog; finish off: one sc.

Size Large ONLY

Row 1: With one strand of Color B and Color D, ch 1, do **not** turn; beginning in same st as joining, sc2tog twice, sc in next 8 sc across, sc2tog twice, leave remaining sc unworked: 12 sc.

Row 2: Ch 1, turn; beginning in first sc, sc2tog twice, sc in next 4 sc, sc2tog twice: 8 sc.

Row 3: Ch 1, turn; beginning in first sc, sc2tog 4 times: 4 sc.

Row 4: Ch 1, turn; beginning in first sc, sc2tog twice: 2 sc.

Row 5: Ch 1, turn; beginning in first sc, sc2tog; finish off: one sc.

FIRST EARFLAP

Row 1: With larger size hook and holding one strand each of Color A and Color C together, skip next 3{3-2} sts from Visor and join yarn with sc in next sc ***(see Joining With Sc, page 29)***; sc in next 6{6-7} sc, leave remaining sc unworked: 7{7-8} sc.

Row 2: Ch 1, turn; sc in each sc across.

Row 3 (Decrease row)**:** Ch 1, turn; beginning in first sc, sc2tog, sc in each sc across to last 2 sc, sc2tog: 5{5-6} sc.

Rows 4-6: Repeat Rows 2 and 3 once, then repeat Row 2 once **more**: 3{3-4} sc.

Size Large ONLY

Row 7: Ch 1, turn; sc in first sc, sc2tog, sc in last sc: 3 sc.

All Sizes

Last Row: Ch 1, turn; beginning in first sc, sc3tog: one sc.

Tie: Ch 14{14-17}, drop previous colors, with one strand each of Color B and Color D together, ch 5, ★ YO, insert hook in fourth ch from hook, YO and pull up a loop, YO and draw through 2 loops on hook; repeat from ★ 3 times **more**, YO and draw all 5 loops on hook, insert hook in same ch, hook Color A and Color C and draw through st and loop on hook, cut Color B and Color D, slip st in each ch across; finish off.

SECOND EARFLAP

With **right** side facing and holding one strand each of Color A and Color C together, skip next 6{6-8} sc from First Earflap, join yarn with sc in next sc; sc in next 6{6-7} sc, leave remaining sc unworked: 7{7-8} sc.

Beginning with Row 2, complete same as First Earflap.

EAR (Make 2)

OUTER EAR

With larger size hook and holding one strand each of Color A and Color C together, ch 6.

Row 1 (Right side)**:** Sc in second ch from hook and in each ch across: 5 sc.

Note: Mark Row 1 as **right** side.

Rows 2-5: Ch 1, turn; sc in each sc across.

Row 6: Ch 1, turn; beginning in first sc, sc2tog, sc in next sc, sc2tog: 3 sc.

Row 7: Ch 1, turn; sc3tog: one sc.

Row 8: Ch 1, turn; sc in sc; finish off.

INNER EAR

With larger size hook and holding one strand each of Color B and Color D together, work same as Outer Ear.

Joining: Hold Inner and Outer Ears with **wrong** sides together and Inner Ear facing. With larger size hook, holding one strand each of Color A and Color C together and working through **both** thicknesses, join yarn with sc in end of Row 1; sc in end of each row across; sc in sc on Row 8; sc in end of each row across; finish off leaving a long end of Color A for sewing.

Using photo as a guide for placement, sew bottom of Ears to Hat.

BUNNY

EASY +

SHOPPING LIST

Yarn (Medium Weight) MEDIUM 4
[3.5 ounces, 170 yards
(100 grams, 156 meters) per skein]:

Scarf

- ☐ Color A (White) - 1 skein
- ☐ Color C (Pink) - 15 yards (13 meters)

Hat

- ☐ Color A (White) - 1 skein
- ☐ Color C (Pink) - 65 yards (59.5 meters)

(Bulky Weight Eyelash) BULKY 5
[1.75 ounces, 64 yards
(50 grams, 58 meters) per skein]:

Scarf

- ☐ Color B (White) - 2 skeins

Hat

- ☐ Color B (White) - 2 skeins

Crochet Hooks

- ☐ Size J (6 mm) **and**
- ☐ Size M/N (9 mm)
  or sizes needed for gauge

Additional Supplies

- ☐ Yarn needle

SIZE INFORMATION

Scarf

Finished Size:
3½" wide x 32½{40-47½}" long/
9 cm x 82.5{101.5-120.5 cm]
and 5" (12.5 cm) width at paws

Hat

Size: Small{Medium-Large}

Fits Head Circumference:
16{18-21}"/40.5{45.5-53.5} cm

Size Note: We have printed the instructions for the sizes in different colors to make it easier for you to find:

- Small in Blue
- Medium in Pink
- Large in Green

Instructions in Black apply to all sizes.

GAUGE INFORMATION

With larger size hook and holding one strand each of Color A and Color B together,
9 sc and 9 rows = 3½" (9 cm)

Gauge Swatch: 3½" (9 cm) square
With larger size hook and holding one strand each of Color A and Color B together, ch 10.

Row 1: Sc in second ch from hook and in each ch across: 9 sc.

Rows 2-9: Ch 1, turn; sc in each sc across.

Finish off.

STITCH GUIDE

SINGLE CROCHET 2 TOGETHER

(abbreviated sc2tog)

Pull up a loop in each of next 2 sc, YO and draw through all 3 loops on hook **(counts as one sc)**.

SINGLE CROCHET 3 TOGETHER

(abbreviated sc3tog)

Pull up a loop in each of next 3 sc, YO and draw through all 4 loops on hook **(counts as one sc)**.

SCARF

With larger size hook and holding one strand each of Color A and Color B together, ch 8.

Row 1: Sc in second ch from hook and in each ch across: 7 sc.

Rows 2-4: Ch 1, turn; 2 sc in first sc, sc in each sc across to last sc, 2 sc in last sc: 13 sc.

Rows 5-12: Ch 1, turn; sc in each sc across.

Rows 13 and 14: Ch 1, turn; sc2tog, sc in each sc across to last 2 sc, sc2tog: 9 sc.

Row 15: Ch 1, turn; sc in each sc across.

Repeat Row 15 until piece measures approximately 27½{35-42½}"/ 70{89-108} cm from beginning ch.

Next 2 Rows: Ch 1, turn; 2 sc in first sc, sc in each sc across to last sc, 2 sc in last sc: 13 sc.

Next 8 Rows: Ch 1, turn; sc in each sc across.

Last 3 Rows: Ch 1, turn; sc2tog, sc in each sc across to last 2 sc, sc2tog: 7 sc.

Finish off.

APPLIQUÉS

LARGE PAD (Make 2)

With smaller size hook and one strand of Color C, ch 7.

Rnd 1 (Right side)**:** Sc in second ch from hook, hdc in next ch, dc in next 2 chs, hdc in next ch, (sc, ch 1, sc) in last ch; working in free loops of beginning ch ***(Fig. 2, page 31)***, hdc in next ch, dc in next 2 chs, hdc in next ch, sc in next ch, ch 1; join with slip st to first sc, finish off leaving a long end for sewing.

Note: Loop a short piece of yarn around any stitch to mark Rnd 1 as **right** side.

SMALL PADS (Make 8)

With smaller size hook and Color C, ch 4.

Rnd 1 (Right side)**:** Sc in second ch from hook, hdc in next ch, sc in last ch, ch 1; working in free loops of beginning ch, sc in next ch, hdc in next ch, sc in next ch, ch 1; join with slip st to first sc, finish off leaving a long end for sewing.

Note: Mark Rnd 1 as **right** side.

Using photo as a guide for placement, page 13, sew one Large Pad with **right** side facing on same side of each end of Scarf. Sew 5 Small Pads with **right** side facing around each Large Pad along outer edge.

HAT

With larger size hook and holding one strand each of Color A and Color B together, work same as Bear Hat, page 4, through First Earflap Row 6{6-7}; do **not** finish off: 3 sc.

All Sizes

Last Row: Ch 1, turn; sc3tog: one sc.

Tie: Ch 15, ★ YO, insert hook in fourth ch from hook, YO and pull up a loop, YO and draw through 2 loops on hook; repeat from ★ 3 times **more**, YO and draw all 5 loops on hook, slip st in same ch and in each ch across; finish off.

SECOND EARFLAP

Row 1: work same as Bear Hat, page 4, through through Row 6{6-7} of Second Earflap; do **not** finish off: 3 sc.

Complete same as First Earflap.

EAR (Make 2)

OUTER EAR

With larger size hook and holding one strand each of MC and CC together, ch 6.

Row 1 (Right side)**:** Sc in second ch from hook and in each ch across: 5 sc.

Note: Mark Row 1 as **right** side.

Rows 2-12: Ch 1, turn; sc in each sc across.

Row 13: Ch 1, turn; sc2tog, sc in next sc, sc2tog: 3 sc.

Row 14: Ch 1, turn; sc in each sc across.

Row 15: Ch 1, turn; sc3tog: one sc.

Row 16: Ch 1, turn; sc in sc; finish off.

INNER EAR

With larger size hook and holding 2 strands of Color A together, work same as Outer Ear.

Joining: Hold Inner and Outer Ears with **wrong** sides together and Inner Ear facing. With larger size hook and holding one strand each of Color A and Color B together, join yarn with sc in end of Row 1; sc in end of each row across; sc in sc on Row 16; sc in end of each row across; finish off leaving a long of Color A end for sewing.

Using photo as a guide for placement, sew bottom 3" (7.5 cm) of Ears to back of Hat.

FROG

EASY

SHOPPING LIST

Yarn (Medium Weight) MEDIUM 4

[3.5 ounces, 170 yards (100 grams, 156 meters) per skein]:

Scarf

- ☐ Green - 2 skeins

Hat

- ☐ Green - 1 skein
- ☐ Black - small amount
- ☐ White - small amount

Crochet Hook

- ☐ Size J (6 mm) **or** size needed for gauge

Additional Supplies

- ☐ Yarn needle

SIZE INFORMATION

Scarf

Finished Size: 3¾{4¾-5¾}" wide x 41¾{45½-45½}" long/ 9.5{12-14.5} cm x 106{115.5-115.5} cm

Hat

Size: Small{Medium-Large}

Fits Head Circumference: 16{18-21}"/ 40.5{45.5-53.5} cm

Size Note: We have printed the instructions for the sizes in different colors to make it easier for you to find:

- Small in Blue
- Medium in Pink
- Large in Green

Instructions in Black apply to all sizes.

GAUGE INFORMATION

In Scarf pattern,
one repeat (12 sts) = 3¾" (9.5 cm)
In Hat pattern,
10 sc and 14 rnds = 4" (10 cm)

Gauge Swatch: 4" (10 cm) square

With Green, ch 11.

Row 1: Sc in second ch from hook and in each ch across: 10 sc.

Rows 2-14: Ch 1, turn; sc in each sc across.

Finish off.

STITCH GUIDE

SINGLE CROCHET 2 TOGETHER ***(abbreviated sc2tog)***

Pull up a loop in each of next 2 sc, YO and draw through all 3 loops on hook **(counts as one sc)**.

SINGLE CROCHET 3 TOGETHER ***(abbreviated sc3tog)***

Pull up a loop in each of next 3 sc, YO and draw through all 4 loops on hook **(counts as one sc)**.

SCARF

With Green, ch 123{135-135}.

Row 1 (Right side)**:** Dc in fourth ch from hook **(3 skipped chs count as first dc, now and throughout)** and in each ch across: 121{133-133} dc.

Note: Loop a short piece of yarn around any stitch to mark Row 1 as **right** side.

Row 2: Ch 1, turn; sc in first dc, ★ ch 11, skip next 11 dc, sc in next dc; repeat from ★ across: 10{11-11} ch-11 sps and 11{12-12} sc.

Row 3: Ch 3 **(counts as first dc, now and throughout)**, turn; (11 dc in next ch-11 sp, dc in next sc) across: 121{133-133} dc.

Rows 4 thru 7{9-11}: Repeat Rows 2 and 3, 2{3-4} times.

Do **not** finish off.

FIRST END EDGING

FIRST LEG

Row 1: Slip st in end of first dc row, ch 8, dc in fourth ch from hook, hdc in next 2 chs, sc in last 2 chs, slip st in end of same row.

Row 2: Ch 1, turn; working in Front Loops Only ***(Fig. 1, page 31)***, sc in first 2 sc, hdc in next 2 hdc, dc in last 2 dc.

Row 3: Ch 3, turn; working in Back Loops Only ***(Fig. 1, page 31)***, dc in next dc, hdc in next 2 hdc, sc in last 2 sc, slip st in end of same dc row.

Second Leg

Row 1: Skip end of next sc row, slip st in end of next dc row, ch 8, dc in fourth ch from hook, hdc in next 2 chs, sc in last 2 chs, slip st in end of same dc row.

Rows 2 and 3: Repeat Rows 2 and 3 of First Leg.

Repeat Second Leg 2{3-4} times.

Finish off.

SECOND END EDGING

FIRST LEG

Row 1: With **right** side facing, join Green with slip st in end of first dc row, ch 8; dc in fourth ch from hook, hdc in next 2 chs, sc in last 2 chs, slip st in end of same row.

Beginning with Row 2 of First Leg complete same as First End Edging.

HAT

With Green, ch 4; join with slip st to form a ring.

Rnd 1 (Right side)**:** Ch 1, 7 sc in ring; join with slip st to first sc.

Note: Mark Rnd 1 as **right** side.

Rnd 2: Ch 1, 2 sc in same st as joining and in each sc around; join with slip st to first sc: 14 sc.

Rnd 3: Ch 1, sc in same st as joining, 2 sc in next sc, (sc in next sc, 2 sc in next sc) around; join with slip st to first sc: 21 sc.

Rnd 4: Ch 1, sc in same st as joining and in next sc, 2 sc in next sc, (sc in next 2 sc, 2 sc in next sc) around; join with slip st to first sc: 28 sc.

Rnd 5: Ch 1, sc in same st as joining and in next 2 sc, 2 sc in next sc, (sc in next 3 sc, 2 sc in next sc) around; join with slip st to first sc: 35 sc.

Rnd 6: Ch 1, sc in same st as joining and in next 3 sc, 2 sc in next sc, (sc in next 4 sc, 2 sc in next sc) around; join with slip st to first sc: 42 sc.

Size Small ONLY

Rnd 7: Ch 1, sc in same st as joining and in next 19 sc, 2 sc in next sc, sc in next 20 sc, 2 sc in last sc; join with slip st to first sc: 44 sc.

Size Medium ONLY

Rnd 7: Ch 1, sc in same st as joining and in next 4 sc, 2 sc in next sc, (sc in next 5 sc, 2 sc in next sc) around; join with slip st to first sc: 49 sc.

Rnd 8: Ch 1, sc in same st as joining, (sc in next 23 sc, 2 sc in next sc) twice; join with slip st to first sc: 51 sc.

Size Large ONLY

Rnd 7: Ch 1, sc in same st as joining and in next 4 sc, 2 sc in next sc, (sc in next 5 sc, 2 sc in next sc) around; join with slip st to first sc: 49 sc.

Rnd 8: Ch 1, sc in same st as joining and in next 5 sc, 2 sc in next sc, (sc in next 6 sc, 2 sc in next sc) around; join with slip st to first sc: 56 sc.

Rnd 9: Ch 1, sc in same st as joining and in next 26 sc, 2 sc in next sc, sc in next 27 sc, 2 sc in last sc; join with slip st to first sc: 58 sc.

All Sizes

Rnd 8{9-10}: Ch 1, sc in same st as joining and in each sc around; join with slip st to first sc.

Next 12{12-14} Rnds: Ch 1, **turn**; sc in each sc around; join with slip st to first sc.

Do **not** finish off.

FIRST EARFLAP

Row 1: Turn; slip st in next 3{4-5} sc, ch 1, sc in same st and in next 10 sc, leave remaining sc unworked: 11 sc.

Row 2: Ch 1, turn; sc in each sc across.

Row 3 (Decrease row)**:** Ch 1, turn; sc2tog, sc in each sc across to last 2 sc, sc2tog: 9 sc.

Rows 4-10: Repeat Rows 2 and 3, 3 times; then repeat Row 2 once **more**: 3 sc.

Row 11: Ch 1, turn; sc3tog; finish off: one sc.

SECOND EARFLAP

Row 1: With **right** side facing, skip next 16{21-26} sc from First Earflap, join Green with sc in next sc ***(see Joining With Sc, page 31)***; sc in next 10 sc, leave remaining sc unworked: 11 sc.

Beginning with Row 2, complete same as First Earflap.

EDGING

With **right** side facing, join Green with sc same st as joining on last rnd of Hat; ★ sc in each sc across to EarFlap, sc in end of each row of Earflap and in sc on Row 11, ch 18{20-22}, dc in fourth ch from hook, hdc in next 2 chs, sc in next ch, (sc, slip st) in next ch, leave remaining chs unworked; **turn**; skip first slip st, working in Front Loops Only, sc in next 2 sc, hdc in next 2 hdc, dc in last 2 dc, ch 3, **turn**; working in Back Loops Only, dc in next dc, hdc in next 2 hdc, sc in next 2 sc, slip st in same st as last slip st (**frog leg made**), slip st in each skipped ch across, sc in same sc on Row 11, sc in end of each row across Earflap; repeat from ★ once **more**, sc in each sc around; join with slip st to first sc, finish off.

EYE (Make 2)

FRONT

With Black, ch 3; join with slip st to form a ring.

Rnd 1 (Right side)**:** Ch 1, 8 sc in ring; join with slip st to first sc, finish off.

Note: Mark Rnd 1 as **right** side.

Rnd 2: With **right** side facing, join White with sc in same st as joining; sc in same st, 2 sc in each sc around; join with slip st to first sc, finish off: 16 sc.

Rnd 3: With **right** side facing and working in Back Loops Only, join Green with sc in same st as joining; sc in same st and in next sc, (2 sc in next sc, sc in next sc) around; join with slip st to **both** loops of first sc: 24 sc.

Last Row: Ch 1, **turn**; sc in first 6 sc, leave remaining sc unworked, finish off leaving a long end for sewing.

Using photo as a guide for placement, sew Eyes to Hat.

RACCOON

EASY +

SHOPPING LIST

Yarn (Medium Weight) 4

[5 ounces, 251 yards
(142 grams, 230 meters) per skein]:

Scarf

☐ Color A (Taupe) - 1 skein

☐ Color B (Brown) - 1 skein

Hat

☐ Color A (Taupe) - 1 skein

☐ Color B (Brown) - 1 skein

(Bulky Weight Eyelash) 5

Taupe - [1.75 ounces, 64 yards
(50 grams, 58 meters) per skein]:

Brown - [1.5 ounces, 57 yards
(40 grams, 52 meters) per skein]:

Scarf

☐ Color C (Taupe) - 2 skeins

☐ Color D (Brown) - 2 skeins

Hat

☐ Color C (Taupe) - 1 skein

☐ Color D (Brown) - 1 skein

Crochet Hook

☐ Size M/N (9 mm)
or size needed for gauge

Additional Supplies

☐ Yarn needle

SIZE INFORMATION

Scarf

Finished Size: 3{3½-4}" wide x 33¾{41¼-48¾}" long/ 7.5{9-10} cm x 85.5{105-124} cm

Hat

Size: Small{Medium-Large}

Fits Head Circumference: 16{18-21}"/40.5{45.5-53.5} cm

Size Note: We have printed the instructions for the sizes in different colors to make it easier for you to find:

- Small in Blue
- Medium in Pink
- Large in Green

Instructions in Black apply to all sizes.

GAUGE INFORMATION

Holding one strand each of Color A and Color C together,
8 dc = 4" (10 cm);
4 rows = 3¾" (9.5 cm)

Gauge Swatch: 4" wide x 3¾" high (10 cm x 9.5 cm)

Holding one strand each of Color A and Color C together, ch 10.

Row 1: Dc in fourth ch from hook **(3 skipped chs count as first dc)** and in each ch across: 8 dc.

Rows 2-4: Ch 3 **(counts as first dc)**, turn; dc in next dc and in each dc across.

Finish off.

SCARF

Holding one strand each of Color A and Color C together and leaving a long end of Color A for sewing, ch 14{16-18}.

Row 1 (Wrong side)**:** Dc in fourth ch from hook **(3 skipped chs count as first dc)** and in each ch across: 12{14-16} dc.

Note: Loop a short piece of yarn around the **back** of any stitch on Row 1 to mark **right** side.

Rows 2-4: Ch 3 **(counts as first dc, now and throughout)**, turn; dc in next dc and in each dc across; at end of Row 4, change to one strand each of Color B and Color D ***(Fig. 3b, page 31)***.

Do **not** cut previous colors unless specified. Each color is carried loosely along the edge and twisted every other row. The carried yarn will be kept to the **inside** when sewing the seam.

Rows 5-8: Ch 3, turn; dc in next dc and in each dc across; at end of Row 8, change to one strand each of Color A and Color C.

Rows 9-12: Ch 3, turn; dc in next dc and in each dc across; at end of Row 12, change to one strand each of Color B and Color D.

Rows 13 thru 32{40-48}: Repeat Rows 5-12, 2{3-4} times; then repeat Rows 5-8 once **more**; at end of last row, cut Colors B and D.

Last 4 Rows: Ch 3, turn; dc in next dc and in each dc across.

Finish off leaving a long end of Color A for sewing.

Thread yarn needle with long end on last row. Weave needle through sts ***(Fig. 5, page 31)***; pull tightly to close and secure end, do **not** cut yarn.

Fold Scarf lengthwise with **wrong** side together; with same yarn, sew seam, matching rows and keeping carried yarn to the inside of piece.

Thread yarn needle with long beginning end. Weave needle through free loops of beginning ch ***(Fig. 2, page 31)***, pull tightly to close and secure end.

HAT

Holding one strand each of Color A and Color C together, ch 4; join with slip st to form a ring.

Rnd 1 (Right side)**:** Ch 1, 8 sc in ring; join with slip st to first sc.

Note: Mark Rnd 1 as **right** side.

Rnd 2: Ch 1, 2 sc in same st as joining and in each sc around; join with slip st to first sc: 16 sc.

Rnd 3: Ch 1, sc in same st as joining, 2 sc in next sc, (sc in next sc, 2 sc in next sc) around; join with slip st to first sc: 24 sc.

Rnd 4: Ch 1, sc in same st as joining and in next sc, 2 sc in next sc, (sc in next 2 sc, 2 sc in next sc) around; join with slip st to first sc: 32 sc.

Size Medium ONLY

Rnd 5: Ch 1, sc in same st as joining and in next 6 sc, 2 sc in next sc, (sc in next 7 sc, 2 sc in next sc) around; join with slip st to first sc: 36 sc.

Size Large ONLY

Rnd 5: Ch 1, sc in same st as joining and in next 2 sc, 2 sc in next sc, (sc in next 3 sc, 2 sc in next sc) around; join with slip st to first sc: 40 sc.

Rnd 6: Ch 1, sc in same st as joining and in next 8 sc, 2 sc in next sc, (sc in next 9 sc, 2 sc in next sc) around; join with slip st to first sc: 44 sc.

All Sizes

Rnd 5{6-7}: Ch 1, sc in same st as joining and in each sc around; join with slip st to first sc.

Next 6{7-8} Rnds: Ch 1, **turn**; sc in each sc around; join with slip st to first sc.

Finish off.

TAIL

Holding one strand each of Color A and Color C together and leaving a long end of Color A for sewing, ch 10{12-14}.

Row 1 (Right side)**:** Dc in fourth ch from hook **(3 skipped chs count as first dc)** and in each ch across: 8{10-12} dc.

Note: Mark Row 1 as **right** side.

Row 2: Ch 3, turn; dc in next dc and in each dc across changing to one strand each of Color B and Color D.

Do **not** cut previous colors unless specified. Each color is carried loosely along the edge and will be kept to the **inside** when sewing the seam.

Rows 3 and 4: Ch 3, turn; dc in next dc and in each dc across; at end of Row 4, change to one strand each of Color A and Color C.

Rows 5 and 6: Ch 3, turn; dc in next dc and in each dc across; at end of Row 6, change to one strand each of Color B and Color D.

Rows 7-13: Repeat Rows 3-6 once, then repeat Rows 3-5 once **more**; at end of Row 13, cut Colors B and D.

Row 14: Ch 3, turn; dc in next dc and in each dc across; finish off leaving a long end of Color A for sewing.

Thread yarn needle with long end on last row. Weave needle through sts; pull tightly to close and secure end, do **not** cut yarn.

Fold Tail lengthwise with **wrong** side together, sew seam matching rows and keeping carried yarn to the inside of piece.

Thread yarn needle with long beginning end. Weave needle through free loops of beginning ch; pull tightly to close and secure end, do **not** cut yarn.

With same yarn, sew Tail to center back of Hat.

SKUNK

EASY +

SHOPPING LIST

Yarn (Medium Weight) MEDIUM 4

[3.5 ounces, 170 yards

(100 grams, 156 meters) per skein]:

Scarf

- ☐ Color A (Black) - 1 skein
- ☐ Color B (White) - 1 skein

Hat

- ☐ Color A (Black)- 1 skein
- ☐ Color B (White) - 1 skein
- ☐ Color E (Pink) - 1 skein

(Bulky Weight Eyelash) BULKY 5

[1.75 ounces, 64 yards

(50 grams, 58 meters) per skein]:

Scarf

- ☐ Color C (Black) - 2 skeins
- ☐ Color D (White) - 2 skeins

Hat

- ☐ Color C (Black) - 2 skeins
- ☐ Color D (White) - 2 skeins

Crochet Hook

- ☐ Size M/N (9 mm)

  or size needed for gauge

Additional Supplies

- ☐ Yarn needle

SIZE INFORMATION

Scarf

Finished Size: 4" wide x 48½{52½-56}" long/ 10 cm x 123{133.5-142} cm

Hat

Size: Small{Medium-Large}

Fits Head Circumference: 16{18-21}"/40.5{45.5-53.5} cm

Size Note: We have printed the instructions for the sizes in different colors to make it easier for you to find:

- Small in Blue
- Medium in Pink
- Large in Green

Instructions in Black apply to all sizes.

GAUGE INFORMATION

Holding one strand each of Color A and Color C together,

8 dc = 4" (10 cm);

6 rows = 5½" (14 cm)

Gauge Swatch: 4" wide x 5½" high (10 cm x 14 cm)

Holding one strand each of Color A and Color C together, ch 10.

Row 1: Dc in fourth ch from hook **(3 skipped chs count as first dc)** and in each ch across: 8 dc.

Rows 2-6: Ch 3 **(counts as first dc)**, turn; dc in next dc and in each dc across.

Finish off.

STITCH GUIDE

SINGLE CROCHET 2 TOGETHER ***(abbreviated sc2tog)***

Pull up a loop in each of next 2 sc, YO and draw through all 3 loops on hook **(counts as one sc)**.

SINGLE CROCHET 3 TOGETHER ***(abbreviated sc3tog)***

Pull up a loop in each of next 3 sts, YO and draw through all 4 loops on hook **(counts as one sc)**.

DOUBLE CROCHET 2 TOGETHER ***(abbreviated dc2tog)*** (uses next 2 dc)

★ YO, insert hook in **next** dc, YO and pull up a loop, YO and draw through 2 loops on hook; repeat from ★ once **more**, YO and draw through all 3 loops on hook **(counts as one dc)**.

SCARF

Holding one strand each of Color A and Color C together and leaving a long end of Color A for sewing, ch 99{107-114}.

Row 1 (Wrong side)**:** Dc in fourth ch from hook **(3 skipped chs count as first dc)** and in each ch across: 97{105-112} dc.

Note: Loop a short piece of yarn around **back** of any stitch on Row 1 to mark **right** side.

Rows 2 and 3: Ch 3 **(counts as first dc, now and throughout)**, turn; dc in next dc and in each dc across; at end of Row 3, change to one strand each of Color B and Color D ***(Fig. 3b, page 31)***, cut previous colors.

Rows 4-6: Ch 3, turn; dc in next dc and in each dc across; at end of Row 6, change to one strand each of Color A and Color C, cut previous colors.

Rows 7-9: Ch 3, turn; dc in each dc across.

Joining Row: Ch 1, with **right** side together and working through both loops of dc on Row 9 **and** in free loops of beginning ch ***(Fig. 2, page 31)***; slip st in each st across; finish off leaving a long end of Color A for sewing.

Thread yarn needle with long end. Weave needle through ends of rows ***(Fig. 5, page 31)***, pull tightly to close and secure end.

Thread yarn needle with long beginning end. Weave needle through ends of rows; pull tightly to close and secure end.

HAT

Holding one strand each of Color A and Color C together, ch 4; join with slip st to form a ring.

Rnd 1 (Right side)**:** Ch 3, 6 dc in ring; join with slip st to first dc: 7 dc.

Note: Mark Rnd 1 as **right** side.

Rnd 2: Ch 3, 2 dc in same st as joining and in each dc around; join with slip st to first dc: 14 dc.

Rnd 3: Ch 3, 2 dc in next dc, (dc in next dc, 2 dc in next dc) around; join with slip st to first dc: 21 dc.

Rnd 4: Ch 3, dc in next dc, 2 dc in next dc, (dc in next 2 dc, 2 dc in next dc) around; join with slip st to first dc: 28 dc.

Size Small ONLY

Rnd 5: Ch 3, dc in next 5 dc, 2 dc in next dc, (dc in next 6 dc, 2 dc in next dc) around; join with slip st to first dc: 32 dc.

Size Medium ONLY

Rnd 5: Ch 3, dc in next 2 dc, 2 dc in next dc, (dc in next 3 dc, 2 dc in next dc) around; join with slip st to first dc: 35 dc.

Rnd 6: Ch 3, dc in next dc and in each dc around to last dc, 2 dc in last dc; join with slip st to first dc: 36 dc.

Size Large ONLY

Rnd 5: Ch 3, dc in next 2 dc, 2 dc in next dc, (dc in next 3 dc, 2 dc in next dc) around; join with slip st to first dc: 35 dc.

Rnd 6: Ch 3, dc in next 3 dc, 2 dc in next sc, (dc in next 4 dc, 2 dc in next dc) around; join with slip st to first dc: 42 dc.

All Sizes

Rnd 6{7-7}: Ch 3, dc in next dc and in each dc around; join with slip st to first dc.

Rnds 7{8-8} thru 8{10-12}: Ch 3, **turn**; dc in next dc and in each dc around; join with slip st to first dc.

Do **not** finish off.

FIRST EARFLAP

Row 1: Slip st in next 5{5-6} dc, ch 3, dc in next 6{6-8} dc, leave remaining dc unworked: 7{7-9} dc.

Row 2: Ch 3, turn; dc in next dc and in each dc across.

Row 3: Ch 3, turn; dc2tog, dc in next dc and in each dc across to last 3 dc, dc2tog, dc in last dc: 5{5-7} dc.

Row 4: Ch 3, turn; dc in next dc and in each dc across.

Row 5: Ch 3, turn; dc2tog 2{2-3} times: 3{3-4} dc.

Sizes Small & Medium ONLY

Row 6: Ch 1, turn; beginning in first sc, sc3tog; finish off: one sc.

Size Large ONLY

Row 6: Ch 1, beginning in first dc, sc3tog, sc in last dc: 2 sc.

Row 7: Ch 1, turn; beginning in first sc, sc2tog; finish off: one sc.

SECOND EARFLAP

Row 1: With **right** side facing and holding one strand each of Color A and Color C together, skip next 10{14-14} dc from First Earflap, join yarn with dc in next dc *(**see Joining With Dc, page 29**)*; dc in next 6{6-8} dc, leave remaining dc unworked: 7{7-8} dc.

Beginning with Row 2, complete same as First Earflap.

EDGING & TIES

With **right** side facing and holding one strand each of Color A and Color C together, join yarn with sc in dc at center back of Hat; sc in each dc across to Earflap; † sc evenly across ends of rows of Earflap, sc in sc on last row, ch 16{18-20}, dc in fourth ch from hook and in each ch across, sc in same st as last sc made, sc evenly across ends of rows †, sc in each dc across to next Earflap, repeat from † to † once, sc in each dc across; join with slip st to first sc, finish off.

EAR (Make 2)

OUTER EAR

Holding one strand each of Color A and Color C together, ch 6.

Row 1 (Right side)**:** Sc in second ch from hook and in each ch across: 5 sc.

Note: Mark Row 1 as **right** side.

Rows 2-4: Ch 1, turn; sc in each sc across.

Row 5: Ch 1, turn; beginning in first sc, sc2tog, sc in next sc, sc2tog: 3 sc.

Row 6: Ch 1, turn; sc in each sc across.

Row 7: Ch 1, turn; beginning in first sc, sc3tog: one sc.

Row 8: Ch 1, turn; sc in sc; finish off.

INNER EAR

Holding two strands of Color E together, work same as Outer Ear.

Joining: Hold Inner and Outer Ears with **wrong** sides together and Inner Ear facing. Holding one strand each of Color A and Color C together, working through both thicknesses and in free loops of beginning ch, join yarn with sc in ch at base of first sc; sc in same st and in next 3 chs, 3 sc in last ch; sc in end of each row across; 3 sc in sc on Row 8; sc in end of each row across and in same ch as first sc; finish off leaving a long end for sewing.

Using photo as a guide for placement, page 21, sew bottom of Ears to Hat.

STRIPE

Holding one strand each of Color B and Color D together, ch 3; join with slip st to form a ring.

Rnd 1 (Right side)**:** Ch 3, 6 dc in ring; join with slip st to first dc: 7 dc.

Note: Mark Rnd 1 as **right** side.

Rnd 2: Ch 3, dc in same st as joining, 2 dc in next dc and in each dc around; join with slip st to first dc: 14 dc.

Rnd 3: Ch 3, 2 dc in next dc, (dc in next dc, 2 dc in next dc) around; join with slip st to first dc: 21 dc.

Rnd 4: Ch 3, dc in next dc, 2 dc in next dc, (dc in next 2 dc, 2 dc in next dc) around; join with slip st to first dc: 28 dc.

Size Large ONLY

Rnd 5: Ch 3, dc in next 2 dc, 2 dc in next dc, (dc in next 3 dc, 2 dc in next dc) around; join with slip st to first dc: 35 dc.

All Sizes

Row 1: Ch 3, dc in next 11{11-13} dc: 12{12-14} dc.

Rows 2 thru 4{6-6}: Ch 3, turn; dc in next dc and in each dc across.

Row 5{7-7}: Ch 1, turn; sc in each dc across.

Row 6{8-8}: Ch 1, turn; beginning in first sc, sc2tog twice, sc in each sc aross to last 4 sc, sc2tog twice: 8{8-10} sc.

Row 7{9-9}: Ch 1, turn; beginning in first sc, sc2tog 4{4-5} times: 4{4-5} sc.

To consolidate the length of a pattern, zeros are sometimes used so that all sizes can be combined. For example, sc in last 0{0-1} sc means the first two sizes would do nothing and the largest size would work a single crochet in last single crochet.

Row 8{10-10}: Ch 1, turn; beginning in first sc, sc2tog twice, sc in last 0{0-1} sc: 2{2-3} sc.

Row 9{11-11}: Ch 1, turn; beginning in first sc, sc2tog{sc2tog-sc3tog}: one sc.

Row 10{12-12}: Ch 1, turn; sc in sc.

Trim: Ch 1, sc evenly around entire piece, working 3 sc in sc on last row; join with slip st to first sc, finish off leaving a long end of Color B for sewing.

Sew Stripe to center back of Hat.

PIG

EASY

SHOPPING LIST

Yarn (Medium Weight) 4

[3.5 ounces, 170 yards (100 grams, 156 meters) per skein]:

Scarf

- ☐ Pink - 2 skeins

Cowl

- ☐ Pink - 1 skein

Hat

- ☐ Pink - 1 skein
- ☐ Black - small amount

Crochet Hook

- ☐ Size J (6 mm) **or** size needed for gauge

Additional Supplies

- ☐ Yarn needle
- ☐ Polyester fiberfill (for Snout)

SIZE INFORMATION

Scarf

Finished Size:

5¼" wide x 52¾{55¼-57¾}" long/ 13.5 cm x 134{140.5-146.5} cm excluding Trim

Cowl

Finished Size:

5¼" wide x 26{28½-31}" circumference/13.5 cm x 66{72.5-79} cm excluding Trim

Hat

Size: Small{Medium-Large}

Fits Head Circumference:

16{18-21}"/40.5{45.5-53.5} cm

Size Note: We have printed the instructions for the sizes in different colors to make it easier for you to find:

- Small in Blue
- Medium in Pink
- Large in Green

Instructions in Black apply to all sizes.

GAUGE INFORMATION

11 dc and 6 rows = 4" (10 cm)

Gauge Swatch: 4" (10 cm) square

With Pink, ch 13.

Row 1: Dc in fourth ch from hook **(3 skipped chs count as first dc)** and in each ch across: 11 dc.

Rows 2-6: Ch 3 **(counts as first dc)**, turn; dc in next dc and in each dc across.

Finish off.

STITCH GUIDE

SINGLE CROCHET 2 TOGETHER *(abbreviated sc2tog)*

Pull up a loop in each of next 2 sc, YO and draw through all 3 loops on hook **(counts as one sc)**.

SINGLE CROCHET 3 TOGETHER *(abbreviated sc3tog)*

Pull up a loop in each of next 3 sc, YO and draw through all 4 loops on hook **(counts as one sc)**.

SCARF

With Pink, ch 136{143-150}.

Row 1 (Right side)**:** Dc in fourth ch from hook **(3 skipped chs count as first dc)** and in each ch across: 134{141-148} dc.

Note: Loop a short piece of yarn around any stitch to mark Row 1 as **right** side.

Rows 2-8: Ch 3 **(counts as first dc, now and throughout)**, turn; dc in next dc and in each dc across.

Do **not** finish off.

TRIM

† Ch 8, turn; sc in second ch from hook and in each ch across, ★ slip st in next 7 sts, ch 8, sc in second ch from hook and in each ch across; repeat from ★ across; working in ends of rows, slip st in first row, ch 8, sc in second ch from hook and in each ch across †, ♥ slip st in same row and in next row, ch 8, sc in second ch from hook and in each ch across ♥; repeat from ♥ to ♥ across, slip st in same row as last slip st; working in free loops of beginning ch ***(Fig. 2, page 31)***, repeat from † to † once; then repeat from ♥ to ♥ across, slip st in same row as last slip st; finish off.

COWL

With Pink, ch 73{80-87}.

Row 1 (Right side)**:** Dc in fourth ch from hook **(3 skipped chs count as first dc)** and in each ch across: 71{78-85} dc.

Note: Mark Row 1 as **right** side.

Rows 2-8: Ch 3, turn; dc in next dc and in each dc across.

First Edge Trim: Ch 8, turn; sc in second ch from hook and in each ch across, slip st in next 7 dc, ★ ch 8, sc in second ch from hook and in each ch across, slip st in next 7 dc; repeat from ★ across; finish off.

Second Edge Trim: With **right** side facing and working in free loops of beginning ch ***(Fig. 2, page 31)***, join Pink with slip st in first ch; ★ ch 8, sc in second ch from hook and in each ch across, slip st in next 7 chs; repeat from ★ across; finish off leaving a long end for sewing.

Thread yarn needle with long end, weave short edges of Cowl together ***(Fig. 4, page 31)***.

HAT

With Pink, ch 4; join with slip st to form a ring.

Rnd 1 (Right side)**:** Ch 1, 7 sc in ring; join with slip st to first sc.

Note: Mark Rnd 1 as **right** side.

Rnd 2: Ch 1, 2 sc in same st as joining and in each sc around; join with slip st to first sc: 14 sc.

Rnd 3: Ch 1, sc in same st as joining, 2 sc in next sc, (sc in next sc, 2 sc in next sc) around; join with slip st to first sc: 21 sc.

Rnd 4: Ch 1, sc in same st as joining and in next sc, 2 sc in next sc, (sc in next 2 sc, 2 sc in next sc) around; join with slip st to first sc: 28 sc.

Rnd 5: Ch 1, sc in same st as joining and in next 2 sc, 2 sc in next sc, (sc in next 3 sc, 2 sc in next sc) around; join with slip st to first sc: 35 sc.

Rnd 6: Ch 1, sc in same st as joining and in next 3 sc, 2 sc in next sc, (sc in next 4 sc, 2 sc in next sc) around; join with slip st to first sc: 42 sc.

Size Small ONLY

Rnd 7: Ch 1, sc in same st as joining and in next 19 sc, 2 sc in next sc, sc in next 20 sc, 2 sc in last sc; join with slip st to first sc: 44 sc.

Size Medium ONLY

Rnd 7: Ch 1, sc in same st as joining and in next 4 sc, 2 sc in next sc, (sc in next 5 sc, 2 sc in next sc) around; join with slip st to first sc: 49 sc.

Rnd 8: Ch 1, sc in same st as joining and in next 23 sc, 2 sc in next sc, sc in next 23 sc, 2 sc in last sc; join with slip st to first sc: 51 sc.

Size Large ONLY

Rnd 7: Ch 1, sc in same st as joining and in next 4 sc, 2 sc in next sc, (sc in next 5 sc, 2 sc in next sc) around; join with slip st to first sc: 49 sc.

Rnd 8: Ch 1, sc in same st as joining and in next 5 sc, 2 sc in next sc, (sc in next 6 sc, 2 sc in next sc) around; join with slip st to first sc: 56 sc.

Rnd 9: Ch 1, sc in same st as joining and in next 26 sc, 2 sc in next sc, sc in next 27 sc, 2 sc in last sc; join with slip st to first sc: 58 sc.

All Sizes

Next 11{12-13} Rnds: Ch 1, **turn**; sc in each sc around; join with slip st to first sc.

Finish off.

SNOUT

With Pink, ch 4; join with slip st to form a ring.

Rnd 1 (Right side)**:** Ch 1, 6 sc in ring; join with slip st to first sc.

Note: Mark Rnd 1 as **right** side.

Rnd 2: Ch 1, 2 sc in same st as joining and in each sc around; join with slip st to first sc: 12 sc.

Rnd 3: Ch 1, sc in same st as joining, 2 sc in next sc, (sc in next sc, 2 sc in next sc) around; join with slip st to first sc: 18 sc.

Rnd 4: Ch 1, sc in Back Loop Only of same st as joining and each sc around *(Fig. 1, page 31)*; join with slip st to first sc.

Rnd 5: Ch 1, **turn**; sc in each sc around; join with slip st to first sc, finish off leaving a long end for sewing.

Thread needle with long end and sew Snout to center front of Hat, stuffing lightly with polyester fiberfill before closing.

EAR (Make 2)

With Pink, ch 6.

Row 1 (Right side)**:** Sc in second ch from hook and in each ch across: 5 sc.

Note: Mark Row 1 as **right** side.

Rows 2 and 3: Ch 1, turn; sc in each sc across.

Row 4: Ch 1, turn; beginning in first sc, sc2tog, sc in next sc, sc2tog: 3 sc.

Row 5: Ch 1, turn; sc in each sc across.

Row 6: Ch 1, turn; beginning in first sc, sc3tog: one sc.

Row 7: Ch 1, turn; sc in sc; finish off.

Trim: With **right** side facing, join Pink with sc in end of Row 1; sc in end of each row across; 3 sc in sc on Row 7; sc in end of each row across; finish off leaving long end for sewing.

Using photo as a guide for placement, sew bottom of Ears to Hat.

EYE (Make 2)

With Black, ch 3; join with slip st to form a ring.

Rnd 1 (Right side)**:** Ch 1, 8 sc in ring; join with slip st to first sc, finish off leaving a long for sewing.

Note: Mark Rnd 1 as **right** side.

Using photo as a guide for placement, sew Eyes to Hat.

TAIL

With Pink, ch 15.

Row 1: Sc in second ch from hook and in each ch across; finish off leaving a long end for sewing: 14 sc.

Using photo as a guide for placement, sew Tail to center back of Hat.

GENERAL INSTRUCTIONS

ABBREVIATIONS

CC	Contrasting Color
ch(s)	chain(s)
cm	centimeters
dc	double crochet(s)
dc2tog	double crochet 2 together
dtr	double treble crochet(s)
hdc	half double crochet(s)
MC	Main Color
mm	millimeters
Rnd(s)	Round(s)
sc	single crochet(s)
sc2tog	single crochet 2 together
sc3tog	single crochet 3 together
sp(s)	space(s)
st(s)	stitch(es)
YO	yarn over

SYMBOLS & TERMS

★ — work instructions following ★ as many **more** times as indicated in addition to the first time.

† to † **or** ♥ to ♥ — work all instructions from first † to second † **or** from first ♥ to second ♥ **as many** times as specified.

( ) or **[ ]** — work enclosed instructions **as many** times as specified by the number immediately following **or** work all enclosed instructions in the stitch or space indicated **or** contains explanatory remarks.

colon (:) — the number(s) given after a colon at the end of a row or round denote(s) the number of stitches or spaces you should have on that row or round.

CROCHET TERMINOLOGY		
UNITED STATES		INTERNATIONAL
slip stitch (slip st)	=	single crochet (sc)
single crochet (sc)	=	double crochet (dc)
half double crochet (hdc)	=	half treble crochet (htr)
double crochet (dc)	=	treble crochet (tr)
treble crochet (tr)	=	double treble crochet (dtr)
double treble crochet (dtr)	=	triple treble crochet (ttr)
triple treble crochet (tr tr)	=	quadruple treble crochet (qtr)
skip	=	miss

GAUGE

Exact gauge is **essential** for proper size. Before beginning your project, make the sample swatch given in the individual instructions in the yarn and hook specified. After completing the swatch, measure it, counting your stitches and rows carefully. If your swatch is larger or smaller than specified, **make another, changing hook size to get the correct gauge**. Keep trying until you find the size hook that will give you the specified gauge.

JOINING WITH SC

When instructed to join with sc, begin with a slip knot on hook. Insert hook in stitch indicated, YO and pull up a loop, YO and draw through both loops on hook.

JOINING WITH DC

When instructed to join with dc, begin with a slip knot on hook. YO, holding loop on hook, insert hook in stitch or space indicated, YO and pull up a loop (3 loops on hook), (YO and draw through 2 loops on hook) twice.

CROCHET HOOKS																	
U.S.	B-1	C-2	D-3	E-4	F-5	G-6	7	H-8	I-9	J-10	K-10½	L-11	M/N-13	N/P-15	P/Q	Q	S
Metric - mm	2.25	2.75	3.25	3.5	3.75	4	4.5	5	5.5	6	6.5	8	9	10	15	16	19

BEGINNER	Projects for first-time crocheters using basic stitches. Minimal shaping.
EASY	Projects using yarn with basic stitches, repetitive stitch patterns, simple color changes, and simple shaping and finishing.
INTERMEDIATE	Projects using a variety of techniques, such as basic lace patterns or color patterns, mid-level shaping and finishing.
EXPERIENCED	Projects with intricate stitch patterns, techniques and dimension, such as non-repeating patterns, multi-color techniques, fine threads, small hooks, detailed shaping and refined finishing.

Yarn Weight Symbol & Names	LACE 0	SUPER FINE 1	FINE 2	LIGHT 3	MEDIUM 4	BULKY 5	SUPER BULKY 6	JUMBO 7
Type of Yarns in Category	Fingering, size 10 crochet thread	Sock, Fingering, Baby	Sport, Baby	DK, Light Worsted	Worsted, Afghan, Aran	Chunky, Craft, Rug	Super Bulky, Roving	Jumbo, Roving
Crochet Gauge* Ranges in Single Crochet to 4" (10 cm)	32-42 sts**	21-32 sts	16-20 sts	12-17 sts	11-14 sts	8-11 sts	6-9 sts	5 sts and fewer
Advised Hook Size Range	Steel*** 6 to 8, Regular hook B-1	B-1 to E-4	E-4 to 7	7 to I-9	I-9 to K-10½	K-10½ to M/N-13	M/N-13 to Q	Q and larger

*GUIDELINES ONLY: The chart above reflects the most commonly used gauges and hook sizes for specific yarn categories.

** Lace weight yarns are usually crocheted with larger hooks to create lacy openwork patterns. Accordingly, a gauge range is difficult to determine. Always follow the gauge stated in your pattern.

*** Steel crochet hooks are sized differently from regular hooks–the higher the number, the smaller the hook, which is the reverse of regular hook sizing.

BACK OR FRONT LOOPS ONLY

Work only in loop(s) indicated by arrows *(Fig. 1)*.

Fig. 1

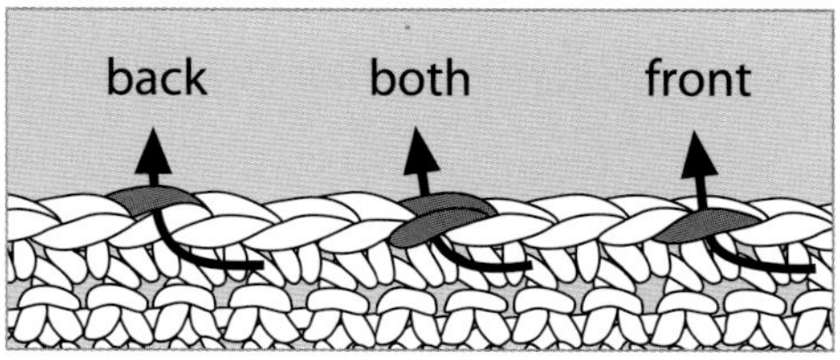

FREE LOOPS OF A CHAIN

When instructed to work in free loops of a chain, work in loop indicated by arrow *(Fig. 2)*.

Fig. 2

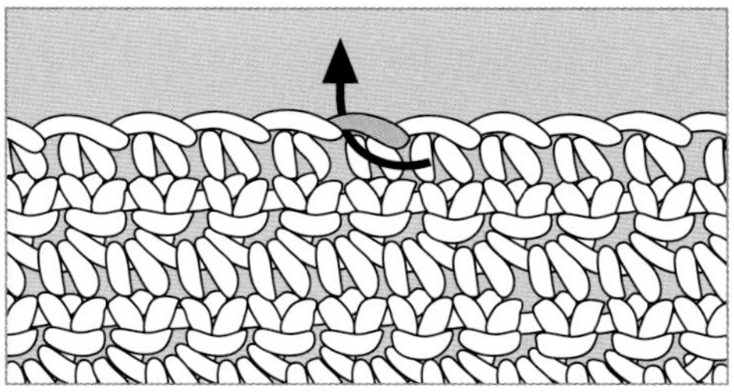

CHANGING COLORS

Work the last stitch to within one step of completion, drop yarn, hook new yarn *(Fig. 3a or Fig. 3b)* and draw through both loops on hook. Do **not** cut old color unless indicated.

Fig. 3a

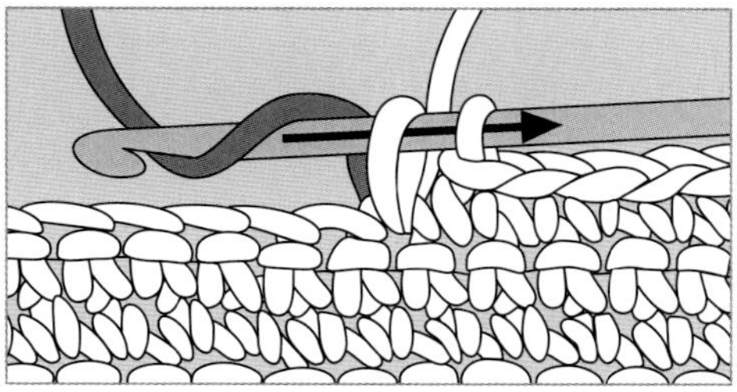

Fig. 3b

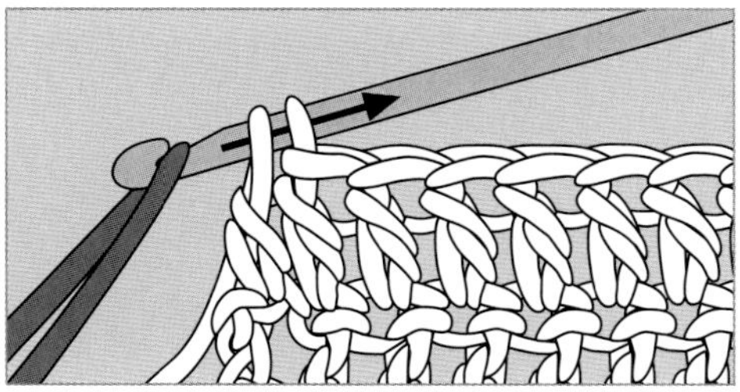

WEAVING SEAMS

With the **right** side facing you and edges even, sew through **both** sides once to secure the seam, leaving an ample yarn end to weave in later. Insert the needle from **right** to **left** through one strand on each piece *(Fig. 4)*. Bring the needle around and insert it from **right** to **left** through the next strands on both pieces. Continue in this manner, drawing seam together as you work.

Fig. 4

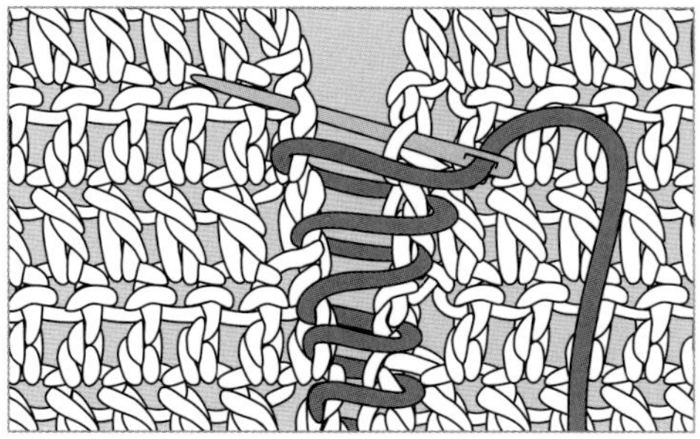

WEAVE THRU STITCHES

Thread yarn needle with long end and weave it through the stitches on the last round *(Fig. 5)*.

Fig. 5

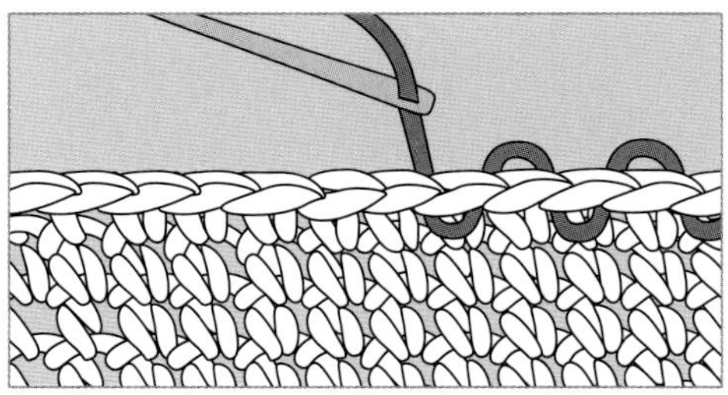

YARN INFORMATION

The projects in this book were made using a variety of yarn weights. Any brand of the specified weight of yarn may be used. It is best to refer to the yardage/meters when determining how many balls or skeins to purchase. Remember, to arrive at the finished size, it is the GAUGE/TENSION that is important, not the brand of yarn.

For your convenience, listed below are specific yarns used to create our photography models. Because yarn manufacturers make frequent changes in their product lines, you may sometimes find it necessary to use a substitute yarn or to search for the discontinued product at alternate suppliers (locally or online).

BEAR SET
Lion Brand® Heartland®
MC (Brown) - #124 Big Bend
Lion Brand® Fun Fur®
CC (Brown) - #126 Chocolate

FOX SET
Lion Brand® Vanna's Choice®
Color A (Orange) - #134 Terracotta
Color B (White) - #100 White
Lion Brand® Fun Fur®
Color C (Orange) - #135 Terracotta
Color D (White) - #100 White

BUNNY SET
Lion Brand® Vanna's Choice®
MC (White) - #100 White
Lion Brand® Vanna's Choice® Baby
Color A (Pink) - #138 Pink Poodle
Lion Brand® Fun Fur®
CC (White) - #100 White

FROG SET
Lion Brand® Vanna's Choice®
Green - #171 Fern
Black - #153 Black
White - #100 White

RACCOON SET
Lion Brand® Heartland®
Color A (Taupe) - #125 Mammoth Cave
Color B (Brown) - #130 Bryce Canyon
Lion Brand® Fun Fur®
Color C (Taupe) - #127 Taupe
Color D (Brown) - #217 Café

SKUNK SET
Lion Brand® Vanna's Choice®
Color A (Black) - #153 Black
Color B (White) - #100 White
Lion Brand® Vanna's Choice® Baby
Color E (Pink) - #138 Pink Poodle
Lion Brand® Fun Fur®
Color C (Black) - #153 Black
Color D (White) - #100 White

PIG SET
Lion Brand® Vanna's Choice® Baby
Pink - #103 Lullabye Pink
Lion Brand® Vanna's Choice®
Black - #153 Black

We have made every effort to ensure that these instructions are accurate and complete. We cannot, however, be responsible for human error, typographical mistakes, or variations in individual work.

Production Team: Technical Writer/Editor - Lois J. Long; Editorial Writer - Susan Frantz Wiles; Senior Graphic Artist - Lora Puls; Graphic Artist - Cailen Cochran; Photo Stylist - Angela Alexander; and Photographer - Jason Masters.